Abiding in the Mountain of God
Survival Strategies for a New Breed of Leaders

LAWRENCE G. RICHARDSON SR.

Outskirts Press, Inc.
Denver, Colorado

The opinions expressed in this manuscript are solely the opinions of the author and do not represent the opinions or thoughts of the publisher. The author represents and warrants that s/he either owns or has the legal right to publish all material in this book.

Abiding in the Mountain of God
Survival Strategies for a New Breed of Leaders
All Rights Reserved.
Copyright © 2008 Lawrence G. Richardson Sr.
V3.0R1.1

Cover Photo © 2008 JupiterImages Corporation. All rights reserved - used with permission.

This book may not be reproduced, transmitted, or stored in whole or in part by any means, including graphic, electronic, or mechanical without the express written consent of the publisher except in the case of brief quotations embodied in critical articles and reviews.

Outskirts Press, Inc.
http://www.outskirtspress.com

ISBN: 978-1-4327-2073-5

Outskirts Press and the "OP" logo are trademarks belonging to Outskirts Press, Inc.

PRINTED IN THE UNITED STATES OF AMERICA

This book is dedicated to my wife Kimberlie. The Bible declared that he that would find a wife would find a good thing and obtain the favor of the Lord (Proverbs 18: 21).

You have done that and so much more!

Time after time during my dark days, you encouraged me to keep going. You always reminded me that I was called to seek the deeper places in the mountain of God!

You would always remind me that I was created for greatness and I was called to prophesy to the nations!

You waited patiently beside me for my new seasons to come. And now my season and time has finally come and I am stepping into destiny more powerful than ever – a lot because of you! While we were waiting, God blessed us with two more wonderful sons to prove that waiting on God was well worth the wait! Together and united we have lived the message "Abiding in the Mountain of God!"

Lawrence G. Richardson, Sr.

Introduction

14 When the Almighty scattered kings in it, it was white as snow in Salmon.
15 A mountain of God is the mountain of Bashan; a mountain of many peaks is the mountain of Bashan.
16 Why do you stare with envy, you mountain of many peaks? This is the mountain which God desires to dwell in; yes the Lord will dwell in it forever. (Psalm 68: 14-16)

In a day of decaying leadership, God now processes a new breed of leaders into and out of the mountain of God. New leaders that shall remind us of days of old when men like Abraham, Moses, and Joshua led the children of Israel into greatness. These new leaders have been assigned to prepare the nations and the kingdoms of this world for the return of Jesus Christ the King. When God finishes the current shift, there will be a great multitude and quality of leaders in the earth unlike any other time in history or any time to come! From the east to the west; from the north to the south; from America to Israel - these God-ordained leaders are now standing and ready to take their place in writing out the final pages in the history of mankind. The fulfilling of Bible prophecy is about to be witnessed in earth through these chosen leaders. They will be on the forefront of every major event leading to the changing of this entire world as it is presently known!

> **1 Blow the trumpet in Zion, and sound an alarm in my holy mountain! Let all the inhabitants of the land tremble; For the day of the Lord is coming, for it is at hand:**
> **2 A day of darkness and gloominess, a day of clouds and thick darkness, like the mourning clouds spread over the mountains, a people come, great and strong, the like of whom has never been; nor will there ever be any such after them, even for many generations. (Joel 2: 1, 2)**

The time has come for these new breed of chosen leaders to rise from obscurity to notoriety. Could you be one of these new breed of leaders? For the last fourteen years, I have listened to God say strange things in the hidden and secret places. I have been writing things heard in quietness that God was saying about a new breed of leaders. This book is being written for those new breed of chosen leaders. I have waited patiently for the right moment to come to release those things I have heard God say. The season and time is here! The moment is right for a new breed of chosen leaders to rise from out of the mountain of God.

There has been and there still exists a clarion call to those that have picked up this book to go into and come out from the mountain of God. You are the new breed of leaders! Please be aware of the many nations and the great kingdoms awaiting you to lead them into the place called the mountain of God.

> **18 For I consider that the sufferings of this present time are not worthy to be compared with the glory which shall be revealed in us.**

19 For the earnest expectation of the creature eagerly waits for the revealing of the sons of God. (Romans 8: 18, 19)

My prayer is that God will speak in such a way to each person holding and reading this book that their lives will never be the same. From here on, those reading will be destined to abide in the mountain of God. While reading, it will become crystal clear that you are one of these chosen leaders that will rise up and begin to rule over nations and kingdoms because of what God did to you while you were abiding in the mountain of God!

Chapter 1

"Transition is here!"

"Men and women make history, and not the other way around. In periods where there is no leadership, society stands still. Progress occurs when skilled leaders seize the opportunity to change things for the better."

Harry S. Truman

1. After the death of Moses the servant of the Lord, it came to pass that the Lord spoke to Joshua the son of Nun, Moses' assistant, saying:
2. Moses My servant is dead. Now therefore, arise, go over this Jordan, you and all this people, to the land which I am giving to them – the children of Israel.
3. Every place that the sole of your foot will tread upon I have given you, as I said to Moses (Joshua 1: 1-3)

The one thing that remains common to most all of mankind is this thing called change. Change being the ability to move from one thing to another. Even if you decide to resist the change, then things around you will continue to change without your cooperation. Everyone is constantly experiencing some type of change. For one, it may be the loss of a dear loved one like Joshua who lost Moses in the afore-mentioned text. And for another reason it may be a minor thing like wearing a new hairstyle that you never dreamed of wearing before. Whether major or minor, everyone will at some point in time have to deal with this thing called change. Change also means to transition from one thing to another. Change entails moving, shifting, passing or surpassing pre-existing and former things. The time is now for the new breed of chosen leaders to embrace change and begin to pass and surpass old landmarks established by the old leadership in the days gone by.

Understand clearly that you will experience change somewhere and at sometime! Understanding that transitioning is a major part of change, you should begin to really seek to understand this thing called transition. Some people go through the processes of transition and come out being the better, while others go through the process of transition and never seem to recover or become the better because of the process of transitioning. Oftentimes, transition is the cause of some people being made worst. They are made worst because much of what is around them may have continued through the process of changing. You transition more effectively when you allow the process called change to bring you right into God's perfect timing and right season. This is the transition that causes you to arrive in the exact place you have been destined to dwell in. This is you becoming exactly what God predestined you to be.

18 But we all, with unveiled face, beholding as in a mirror the glory of the Lord, are being transformed into the same image from glory to glory, just as by the spirit of the Lord. (II Corinthians 3: 18)

Transitions are necessary for a chosen leader to go through in order to arrive at their God-ordained destinies. For each of you reading this book, especially since you are one of the new breed of chosen leaders, there will be a season of transition mandatory for you to mature into everything that God predestined you to be. Your destiny becomes clearer as you matriculate through this season of transition. If you are to become that which God has ordained you to be then these transitions must be embraced and never resisted. Transitions are the most important part of the evolutionary process in you becoming the leader God has chosen and destined you to be. Often, it will of take place in the mountain of God. While abiding there, you are changed forever!

In this writing, the main point you should understand is that God is causing a transitioning in the leadership of His chosen people called the Church or Body of Christ. As He did with Moses and Joshua in chapter one of the Book of Joshua, God transitioned His new breed of chosen leaders. God did this with Moses and Joshua in leading them out of the wilderness. Now God is ready to lead His Church out of the wilderness. Again, He is passing the baton from Moses to Joshua! God has determined that the time is now for a new breed of chosen leaders to rise.

In this writing, I will focus mainly on God's people and spiritual leadership being the major examples. However, many of the statements, concepts and principles apply to leaders across all lines and in most scopes of leadership. God is going to use this leadership change to release a new breed of chosen leaders in all parts of society. These leaders will establish and place Godly principles and concepts in all the places they are given opportunity to lead, especially in societies where great moral failure has occurred!

In times passed, God transitioned an entire group of failing leaders under the leadership of Moses. The failing group following Moses, God transitioned out, and a new group following Joshua, He transitioned in. Through Joshua's leadership they became great conquerors. How could this possibly happen with the change of one leader – Moses to Joshua? Prayerfully, you will come to a reasonable answer after reading the remainder of this book. While coming to that answer along the way, you should also gain practical principles for your coming leadership shift. There is one thing you and this group of chosen leaders must master: you must stop repeating the mistakes of leaders that have proceeded before you. No more business as usual! You are a chosen new breed of leaders and you have been born to enter into a brand new day!

In the book of Exodus, Moses is leading a group of God's people from slavery to a new place called Canaan – The Land of Promise! Moses is chosen to lead while the children of Israel are under the cruel hand of Pharaoh and dwelling in tremendous bondage (Exodus 3). Exodus records Israel breaking free from Pharaoh by the strong hand of God and the brave leadership of God's servant Moses.

7 And the Lord said: I have surely seen the oppression of My people who are in Egypt, and have heard their cry because of their taskmasters, for I know their sorrows.
8 So I have come down to deliver them out of the hand of the Egyptians, and to bring them up from that land to a good and large land, to a land flowing with milk and honey, to the place of the Canaanites and the Hittites and the Amorites and the Perizzites and the Hivities and the Jebusites.
9 Now therefore, behold, the cry of the children of Israel has come to Me, and I have also seen the oppression with which the Egyptians oppress them.
10 Come now, therefore, and I will send you to Pharaoh that you may bring My people, the children of Israel, out of Egypt. (Exodus 3: 7-10)

God declares three things in the afore-mentioned text:

I. He has seen the oppression of His chosen people and that the time for it to end had come;
II. He had come down to deliver them out of the hand of the Egyptians; and
III. He chose Moses for leadership of this great work. God alone would accomplish this great work through Moses following only Him.

God proclaimed to Moses that He had been chosen to move these people from the bondage of Egypt to the bountiful and fruitful land of Canaan. However, this group would leave Egypt but they would not enter the promised land of Canaan under the leadership of Moses. Even with God's strong hand being with them, they never entered the promised land of Canaan.

9 It shall be as a sign to you on your hand and as a memorial between your eyes, that the Lord's law may be in your mouth; for with a strong hand hath the Lord has brought you out of Egypt. (Exodus 13: 9)

You have to understand that the children of Israel left Egypt delivered by the strong hand of God! Moses began to lead these people on a great journey through a terrible wilderness. However, they never entered the land of promise and the place of destiny! Along the way, they experienced forty years of wandering around the same mountain and stumbling through the same fiery wilderness. The word "wander" means to move or go about aimlessly, without fixed destination. As you look closely, you begin to discover why this group never moved into the place of destiny called Canaan.

2 All were baptized into Moses in the cloud and in the sea,
3 All ate the same spiritual food,
4 And all drank the same spiritual drink. For they drank of that spiritual Rock that followed them, and that Rock was Christ.
5 But with most of them God was not well pleased, for their bodies were scattered in the wilderness.
6 Now these things became our examples, to the intent that we should not lust after evil things as they also lusted.
7 And do not become idolaters as were some of them. As it is written, the people sat down to eat and drink, and rose up to play.
8 Nor let us commit sexual immorality, as some of them did, and in one day twenty-three thousand fell;
9 Nor let us tempt Christ, as some of them also tempted, and were destroyed by serpents;

10 Nor complain, as some of them complained, and were destroyed by the destroyer.
11 Now all these things happened to them as examples, and they were written for our admonition, upon whom the ends of the ages have come. (I Corinthians 10: 2-11)

This group of people, while coming out of the bondage of Egypt, never discovered the importance of trusting in the Lord God with their entire heart nor the need to totally obey.

In their transition, God expected His people to walk in complete obedience, always being grateful, and coming to a place of living by His statues and commands. This would become the standard for kingdom living. However, they failed in nearly every one of God's expectations. They crumbled under very little pressure when they should have been standing the tallest. They failed to understand that God was in total control and nothing was against them to destroy them if they obeyed and walked faithfully with their God. So, instead of advancing, they wandered for forty long years in the great wilderness.

And yet today, again, there is a group of people that God is not pleased with – they have followed the ways of the children of Israel under the leadership of Moses. There is a group of leaders that are complaining that their automobiles are not large enough; that their houses do not have enough rooms or enough square footage; and that the ministries in which God is birthing in them is not growing fast enough. All the while forgetting where God has already brought them from. There is a group of leaders that also have no sense of Biblical morality. Every day they are moving further away from God and His holy statutes. They are classifying wrong as right and right as wrong.

6 In those days there was no king in Israel; everyone did what was right in his own eyes. (Judges 17: 6)

Because these people no sense of urgency, the present-day leaders are causing the masses to wander into the great wilderness like the children of Israel of old. Of greater importance, these leaders are having a negative effect on too many in the Church already and others that are considering coming into the Church. Since these groups of leaders have no fixed destination, they are leading many away from biblical teaching and the life that would emulate the life of Jesus Christ. Now, too many people in Church, Sunday after Sunday, are living lifestyles that are conformed to this world.

But the devil is a liar! You are the ones that this book was written for – it's time to get up into the mountain of God and watch God begin a new thing in your life and your leadership. In the mountain of God you will be changed for the better and be empowered to complete your God-given assignment and change the tide of the current moment!

Everyone – including you – must go through the place of abiding in the mountain of God! This is where you will become single in your divine purpose. This is the place where the present-day strategies will be birthed. This fresh movement will cause concepts to be understood and cause principles to be applied to everyday living! God shall connect you to your destiny through this move and right into the mountain of God! Since you are ready to move forward into the mountain of God, here are a couple of helpful hints:

- Do not allow anything or any person to prevent you from transitioning from your old ways;
- Release everything and everyone that would hold you in the level you currently occupy;
- Determine that you are now ready to move up and move ahead;
- Make a vow that you will not complain nor become bitter by the path God has chosen for you to take.

Know that transition will not be easy, but it will be doable! God has opened the door that leads you into your change and you transitioning. This move will take you into conquering and occupying your land of promise. Here are a few helpful hints since you are ready to move out into the mountain of God.

- All transitions began with change.
- Listen and look for new instructions.
- Believe, trust, and watch God perform that which He has spoken and even that which He has yet to speak.

Transition is here! You will now move in different timing and to different places. You will even experience the place of death – Jesus called it Calvary. Take courage because with this death experience comes the experience of the power of a resurrected life (Romans 8: 13)! You shall get up! You shall come to the place of peace and rest in the thing that you have been birthed to complete. The mountain of God's experience shall bring forth things never imagined or dreamed. You shall move to doing greater things – once you have come to the season and time of abiding in the mountain of God!

Chapter 2

"Now entering a land of limitless possibilities"

"You can't solve a problem on the same level that it was created. You have to rise above it to the next level."

Albert Einstein

Moses led the children of Israel out of the tiresome bondage of Egypt. Yet Moses could not get this same group of people to go into the place of promise called Canaan. Moses and this group never entered the land that God promised. The Promised Land that flowed with milk and honey was the ultimate destiny for the children of Israel. In this chapter, I will attempt to answer the question of why this occurred. Why did God have to mandate Joshua to replace Moses before the children of Israel could enter the Promise Land? Now again today – why is God changing leadership to a new breed of chosen leaders? If you closely look at the transition of leadership from Moses to Joshua, you discover important principles that assist in guiding you through the transition that has begun in you!

> **12 And the Lord spake unto Moses and Aaron, because ye believed me not, to sanctify me in the eyes of the children of Israel, therefore ye shall not bring this congregation into the land which I have given them. (Numbers 20: 12)**

This great man Moses of signs, wonders, and miracles missed the opportunity to lead the children of Israel into the land of promise. In the defining moment of Moses' leadership, he did not believe God would convince the children of Israel for their divine provisions. In the moment of failing faith, God began the process of replacing Moses with Joshua! God replaced one leader with another to take the children of Israel into the land of promise. Today, God is orchestrating a change in leadership. A fresh new breed of leaders is on the horizon ready to rise out of the mountain of God (Psalm 75: 6, 7).

This fresh breed of emerging leaders will be responsible for empowering many in the Church and a select few in the world back to a relationship with the Almighty God. These leaders will turn the tide and bring morality and Christian values back to a nation in desperate need of revival. These chosen leaders will walk in morality and honor. Their walk will inspire a raised standard of living moral and by Christian values. They will no longer be led by worldly and secular values of mainstream society.

This is the shift that will usher in a new breed of chosen leaders. This will open the door to living in the land of limitless possibilities. When these new leaders take their place, then the Church, nations, and kingdoms will reach their destined level of greatness. All of mankind will be lead into the paths of righteousness, peace, and the joy of living for God.

Take note that your very hearts are now being stirred to turn to or back to the living God. This is happening regardless of your stature in society or your place in the eyes of men. This is a new tug that is going on in your heart to turn to God for guidance and direction. You and much of humanity are becoming hungry for something with better promises and more fulfilling possibilities. The Moses-type leadership of yesterday has led as far as they can lead with limited possibilities. New Joshua's are showing up to usher you into your land of limitless possibilities. God has released your Joshua to take you into a brand new day!

1 **Now after the death of Moses, the servant of the Lord, it came to pass, that the Lord spake unto Joshua the son of Nun saying,**
2 **Moses my servant is dead; now therefore arise, go over this Jordan, thou, and this people, unto the land which I do give to them, even to the children of Israel. (Joshua 1: 1, 2)**

The time is now for you to begin to enter the land of limitless possibilities. You will not just stumble into conquering or occupying this land. God has chosen and called a Joshua-type leader to push you all the way into the land of promise! The living God is up to something that is causing great change. He is moving again as He did in the days of Moses and Joshua – but now it shall be far greater!

> 22 They departed and went to the mountain, and stayed there three days until the pursuers returned. The pursuers sought them all along the way, but did not find them.
> 23 So the two men returned, descended from the mountain, and crossed over; and they came to Joshua the son of Nun, and told him all that had befallen them.
> 24 And they said to Joshua, "Truly the Lord has delivered all the land into our hands, for indeed all the inhabitants of the country are fainthearted because of us. (Joshua 2: 22-24)

This transition from Moses to Joshua changed all of Israel's history. Under the leadership of Joshua, the children of Israel became great conquerors. They moved into living by great faith, experiencing great hope, and always being totally obedient. They moved into the land of limitless possibilities! They gained possession over lands possessed by men of greater stature than themselves.

What once was impossible under the leadership of one became possible under the leadership of another. Joshua demanded the people to obey God and to follow God with their whole heart (Joshua 1: 18)! Joshua caused all the people of his generation to transition into the land of limitless possibilities. It is my prayer that you also will now move into another level as you seize this opportunity to follow the leading of your Joshua!

Joshua comes on the scene with purpose and determination. Joshua arrives before any further failures could occur through Moses or his core of leaders. You will see that God's ways are always perfect and his timing impeccable.

Let's look a bit closer to why Moses had to be replaced. The transition took place mainly because of the following two reasons:

- Leaders in position that were no longer honoring God in their complete obedience;
- Leaders in position that no longer believed the commandments or the capabilities of the true and living God.

The leaders that God takes into greatness are the leaders that honor him with their highest reverence in all they do. This reverence is demonstrated at all times and under all circumstances. These leaders seem to understand the affect their decisions have on the destinies of the rest of mankind. God is always watching and ensuring that His chosen leaders are causing humanity to move right into His predetermined purposes. Whenever God sees that a leader or a group of leaders are not turning from their own ways to His ways, God then begins to arrange for a change to the new breed of chosen leaders.

> 16 For now I have chosen and sanctified this house, that My name may be there forever; and My eyes and My heart will be there perpetually.
> 17 As for you, if you walk before Me as your father David walked, and do according to all that I have commanded you, and if you keep My statues and My judgments.
> 18 Then I will establish the throne of your kingdom as I covenanted with David your father, saying, "You shall not fail to have a man as ruler in Israel."
> 19 But if you turn away and forsake My status and My commandments which I have set before you, and go and serve other gods, and worship them,

20 Then I will uproot them from My land which I have given them; and this house which I have sanctified for My name I will cast out of My sight, and will make it a proverb and a byword among all peoples.
21 And as for this house, which is exalted, everyone who passes by it will be astonished and say, "Why has the Lord done thus to this land and this house?"
22 Then they will answer, "Because they forsook the Lord God of their fathers, who brought them out of the land of Egypt, and embraced other gods, and worshipped them and served them; therefore He as brought all this calamity on them." (II Chronicles 7: 16-22)

Time after time you read and see this pattern repeated in the Bible! God removes wicked and disobedient leaders to be replaced by a new breed of chosen leaders that will obey Him in all their ways! In times past, He replaced wicked kings, wicked judges, and wicked priests. A judge, in the book of I Samuel, and his sons were so wicked that God broke the neck of the judge and named his newly born grandson 'Ichabod,' meaning the glory of the Lord departed (I Samuel 4). God has consistently replaced one leader with another chosen leader that He raised up to go after His ways (Acts 13: 22).

You are going to become one of these new breed of chosen leaders and now you should operate in the following ways because of where you must lead others to:

- You should honor God above all others.
- You should not do your own thing or seek your own agenda.
- You should walk in complete obedience – partial obedience is the same thing as full disobedience.

- You should study the biblical leaders that have gone before you because the history that you do not know will be the history you end up repeating.
- You should always look for the highest level in which you can operate – and always operate there.
- You should know that you possess God-given greatness, divine abilities, and powerful gifting.
- You should be strong and courageous.
- You should never settle for the status quo or average.

It is now time to make a firm decision. It's time for you to lead, follow, or get out of the way! The choice is yours to make. You have been chosen to lead! It is a time for the door leading to the land of limitless possibilities to open. God is looking for those that are ready to move through the open door.

Like the transformation of the wormy insect caterpillar into a beautiful butterfly, you must now transform into the purpose God has destined for you. The caterpillar resembles you prior to transformation – immature and unready for destiny. But the butterfly is what you are becoming, possessing the ability to fly to new lands and greater heights. Once a butterfly, you discover that you are ready to enter and possess the land of limitless possibilities.

> **7 Only be strong and very courageous, that you may observe to do according to all the law which Moses My servant commanded you; do not turn from it to the right hand or the left, that you may prosper wherever you go.**
>
> **8 This Book of the Law shall not depart from your mouth, but you shall meditate in it day and night, that you may observe to do according to all that is written in it. For then you will make your way prosperous, and then you will have**

good success. (Joshua 1: 8, 9)

The door to your promised land is open for you and your leading many others is just ahead. Are you really ready and prepared for this new land and new responsibility? In transitioning to this land, you must pass through the place of dark nights and a high mountain. You have waited patiently and served faithfully. Once you have made it through this land, you will enter a new place of wanting for nothing.

However, the dark night must be navigated successfully through! Then you will be on your way to being complete, established and wanting for nothing (James 1: 4). May the force of God go with you as you move into your land, through the nights, and into abiding in the mountain of God!

Now is the time to move ahead, go out into the night!

Chapter 3

'Journeying Through dark nights'

As we wait upon the Lord, we learn to see things from His perspective, move at His pace, and function under His directives. Waiting times are growing times and learning times. As we quiet our heart, we enter His pace; as we lay down our will, we hear His calling. When we mount up, we are being lifted by the wind of His Spirit. When we move ahead, we are sensitive to His timing. When we act, we give ourselves only to the things He has asked us to do.

Roy Lessin

I want to push you further into the text of Joshua 2. This is the biblical account of the children of Israel entering into another phase. Moses is now dead and the children of Israel are being led by Joshua, the new chosen leader replacing Moses. Joshua takes charge and it is very clear that he is determined not to repeat the mistakes of the former leadership. During Moses' leadership, Israel sent twelve spies to check out the land (Numbers 13); however, here Joshua sends only two spies to view the same land as before!

> **1 And Joshua the son of Nun sent out of Shittim two men to spy out secretly, saying, Go, view the land, especially Jericho. So they went, and came to the house of a harlot named Rahab, and lodged there.**
> **2 And it was told the king of Jericho, saying, behold, men have come here tonight from the children of Israel to search out the country. (Joshua 2: 1, 2)**

These two spies are the prototype of the new breed of chosen leaders coming on the scene today. They are not like the old order of leaders. They represent the rise of a new leadership that begins to direct in a new way. Note the text; they have been sent out to journey into the dark night. Joshua pushes them out of their comfort levels and out of their comfort zone. Can you imagine if this was you being lead from the covering of the camp into the unknown of a dark night? This is like what many of you are presently experiencing. You are being pushed out of your comfort zone into places of the unknown and even darkness.

You are now out in the night and the first thing that catches your attention is the darkness of this present night. Please take comfort this is your first step in transitioning into leadership. Prior to you becoming the leader you are destined to be you must pass through this test of being lost in the night! It is only after squashing the fear of the dark night do leaders pass through and ascend to that safe place in the mountains of God (Zephaniah 3: 17-20)!

Understand that this dark night has been specially designed for each of you. Yes, God has designed it just for you! For one person, the dark night may be a difficult financial struggle or hardship. For another, it may be a great struggle to maintain his or her sexual purity. And yet for another, it may be the isolation of standing all alone for untold seasons. Regardless of how your night has manifested, they are all specially designed nights for each of you. It is purposed to strengthen and establish you for where God has destined you to go. The struggles, battles and victories will strengthen you for all that lies ahead. When your designed night has ended, you will be able to declare you are well able to conquer the land of promise!

There are some distinct purposes for going through dark nights. I will give you others later in this chapter, but first and foremost it is for self-analyzing; then for bringing total submission to all areas of your life; and finally, for convincing you that God will always have His way in your life.

A dark night normally turns into a dark season, rarely going away after the passing of a few moments. Normally, they last for weeks and turn into complete seasons consisting of days, months, and some times years. Once the night begins, you must determine that you will still be standing whenever God chooses for the night to end! Remind yourself of its purpose and determine to survive through no matter how long it may last.

Let's look closer at the true meaning of the word "night." Webster defines night as any period or condition of darkness; a period of intellectual or moral degeneration; time of grief. You and every other chosen to be new-breed leader will inevitably experience a night or night season. God dictates and designs those nights for His chosen leaders. The time will come when God says its time for your purpose to become clear and your vision to be expanded. He then orders one of those dark nights! In this time, you must look through the eyes of faith, and patiently walk through the dark night (II Corinthian 5: 7). Viewing the dark night through the eyes of faith your trust in God will begin to grow. And you will also begin to believe and see that God is causing you to progress through your darkest nights.

In the dark nights, you should come to know that God is working behind the scenes and bringing together what He said He was going to do in your life. At times, God's work cannot be understood from beginning to end (Ecclesiastes 3: 11). In moments of dark nights, your faith and trust in God is being tested and challenged. You must believe God is working everything out for your good (Romans 8: 28).

Be assured in your darkest night that God is going to bring you out (Isaiah 43: 2). Hold on to your faith and to your confession of faith (Psalm 34: 19)! God is faithful even in times of your faithlessness. Look at Jacob's night experience.

22 And he rose up that night; and took his two wives, his two female servants, and his eleven sons, and crossed over the ford of Jabbok.
23 He took them, sent them over the brook, and sent them over the brook, and sent over what he had.
24 Then Jacob was left alone; and a Man wrestled with him until the breaking of day. (Genesis 32: 22-24)

What you should notice in the afore- mentioned text, is the conditions surrounding Jacob's night experience – mainly that he was left all alone with the angel of the Lord. He had shared closeness with he dear wife, but in his darkest night he was left alone even from her. His friends may have been loyal up until this point, but at this moment they had left him alone. His caring father Abraham could not lead him through this part of his designed journey; because the moment arrived when he needed to be left alone.

There are some things you must be aware of once you enter the place of being all alone and discover you are in a dark night. This is the place where it is only you and the darkness of night. But it is, also the entrance to the mountain of God. You have reached the place in which you must choose to go further or choose to turn around. This is the place of transition. You will pass points where others have stopped and gone no further! This is the place where the leaders are separated from the followers. Here, in the depth of a dark night, Jacob wrestled with the angel and his life was changed forever. Every person becoming that new breed of leaders will face this same dark night. Only those of great faith and total trust in the Lord will survive this type of experience and move on forward.

There are two things that the dark nights will bring to every new breed leader, which are the following: first, a place of self-analyzing. The word analyze means to evaluate; to separate into parts or basic principles so as to determine the nature of the whole; examine methodically (Proverbs 19: 21; Psalm 139: 23, 24). When you enter into the dark night you must examine and then re-examine yourself to determine what you are really made of. Who you are determines how you conduct yourself in the night. In the dark night all alone, you will see who you are and prayerfully discover who God is forming you to be. In this unfamiliar place, you discover your true self and things you would have never known if not for the dark night.

The second thing about the dark night is that you're potentially positioned to be corrected of secret sins, repaired from minor defects, and moved beyond other flaws. The word "repair" means to restore to good condition; to bring back to a healthy state; improve. Your God has an uncanny way of checking your condition and makeup. He knows just how to shake your foundation to ensure you are standing as a complete new breed of leader.

> **25 See that you do not refuse Him who speaks. For if they did not escape who refused Him who spoke on earth, much more shall we not escape if we turn away from Him who speaks from heaven,**
> **26 Whose voice then shook the earth; but now He has promised, saying, yet once more I shake not only the earth, but also the heaven.**
> **27 Now this, yet once more, indicates the removal of those things that being shaken, as of things that are made, that the things which cannot be shaken may remain.**
> **28 Therefore, since we are receiving a kingdom which cannot be shaken, let us have grace, by which we may serve God acceptably with reverence and godly fear.**
> **29 For our God is a consuming fire. (Hebrews 12: 25-29)**

It is in the middle of your darkest night you will discover the true condition of your foundation. Look at the condition of Jacob's foundation. He had the stability to wrestle with the angel of the Lord and to prevail. He received a new name signifying a brand new identity. This new name identified who he really is. He emerged out of the dark night having both power with God and being a prince among men (Genesis 32: 28).

Note these following applicable principles:

- When you discover things that may hinder you from going into the promise land, you should be swift to release those things.
- God desires to take you into new places – your cooperation determines His freedom to do so.

- Christ's character being formed in you is a high priority and very important to God.
- When your dark night or dark night season is over you will be changed and empowered to lead a great number of others through their dark night.

Walking through dark nights will change you forever. There is a time and season appointed that you must move on and move ahead. Your mind will be changed into possessing the mind of Jesus Christ. You are refreshed, revived, and sense a higher purpose calling you into more of God's will. God has totally repaired you and you are prepared for what's next!

1 **Come let us return unto the Lord; for He hath torn, but He will heal us; He has stricken, but He will bind us up.**
2 **After two days He will revive us; on the third day He will raise us up, that we may live in His sight,**
3 **Let us know, let us pursue knowledge of the Lord. His going forth is established as the morning; He will come to us like the rain, like the latter and former rain to the earth. (Hosea 6: 1-3)**

The dark night experience was a unique experience for the two spies Joshua sent out to view the land of promise. It will also be a similar experience for you new breed of chosen leaders. In the darkness of night, you all have witnessed the true greatness of your God and the incredible places God is ready to bring you into. God has shown that He is able to make ways for His chosen people even in the midst of what appears to be the shadow of death (Joshua 2: 1-15)!

After the night, Joshua's men returned to the camp knowing that their victory had already been won. And even though they were still in the midst of dark nights, they knew God would somehow make a way out of no way. Coming out of the dark night they were able to tell Joshua, with full confidence, their day of victory was just ahead!

> **22 They departed and went to the mountain, and stayed there three days until the pursuers returned. The pursuers sought them all along the way, but they did not find them.**
> **23 So the two men returned, descended from the mountain, and crossed over; and they came to Joshua the son of Nun, and told him all that had befallen them.**
> **24 And they said to Joshua, truly the Lord has delivered all the land into our hands, for indeed all the inhabitants of the country are fainthearted because of us. (Joshua 2: 22-25)**

The weeping and moving through the night had ended for these two spies and they had transitioned to a greater place of faith. Just like their dark night ended, there will come an ending to your dark nights. After patiently waiting on the Lord, He shall surely deliver you to places of faith and confidence. Release your will that His will may prevail. God is working everything after the counsel of His own will (Ephesians 1: 11). He is using the season of dark nights to do this work and transition you to your next place in Him.

With this night season coming to an end, you will be ready for the blessings of the next place in Him, as you approach the mountain of God. You are witnessing the beauty of the dawning of a new day. The dark night in which you are coming through is a testimony that God has great things in store for you. Many others did not survive through the dark nights. But you are still here. Not only as a survivor, but now you attest that you are more than a conqueror! Just when you are ready to give up and quit, God will show up in the darkest part of the night and begin to work His mighty power and great acts!

In the right time and in the right season, you will exit out of your designed dark night. You should notice that some things have been gained for your good. But some other things have been lost, which also is for your good. You may even notice you have a limp like Jacob did leaving his dark night (Genesis 32: 25). But, you are exiting out of the dark night. Your limp will be your medal of honor. You have prevailed and now you are standing as a new breed of leader. You will be one of the heroes of the faith! You are now walking in a greater glory and a greater anointing. Take your time here to rest and reflect on how far the Lord has brought you.

Rest as long as you can. When you are well rested, it will be time to go forward. Do not forget there still remains a great high mountain – the mountain of God in which you must now come to abide in!

Chapter 4

'The mountain of God'

Then Jacob awoke from his sleep and said, "Surely the Lord is in this place, and I did not know it."

And he was afraid and said, "How awesome is this place! This is none other than the house of God, and this is the gate of heaven!"

(Genesis 28: 16, 17)

23 And they departed and went to the mountain, and stayed there three days until the pursuers returned. The pursers sought them all along the way, but did not find them.
24 So the two men returned, descending from the mountain, and crossed over; and they came to Joshua the son of Nun, and told him all that had befallen them. (Joshua 2: 22, 23)

The mountain these two spies came through is like the mountain of God's habitation (Psalm 68: 14-16). It is a hiding place for God's new breed of leaders while they are in transition. **This is the mountain in which God chooses to take each leader He has chosen for greatness!** It is a mountain of great height and of great depth. God's mountain is both fearful and beautiful although it could appear very intimidating. Nevertheless, it is the mountain of God. It obscures your natural ability to see clearly. While in the mountain, it often appears that you may be lost and will never make your way out of the mountain. It is the mountain of the Lord – God's dwelling place!

Let's explore more about this mountain of the Lord. We will do this by looking at natural mountains, which are a raised part of the earth's surface. When someone goes to climb a mountain, the mountain hides them from the natural eye's view. The mountain climbers may use this place of being hidden to get away from the business of everyday life. God uses His mountain to get His chosen leaders away from everything and everyone during their season of transition.

3 Who may ascend into the hill of the Lord? Or who may stand in His holy place?
4 He who has clean hands and a pure heart, who has not lifted up his soul to an idol, nor sworn deceitfully.

5   He shall receive the blessing from the Lord, and righteousness from the God of his salvation. (Psalm 24: 3-5)

God places leaders into His mountain to reveal to them His new way, His new vision, and release His new anointing. Or just to hide them for a season and a time. I will attempt to explain this to you through one of my real-life experiences.

During a season when I was wondering what was going on with my life and in which direction God was leading me, I looked up and found myself living in the majestic mountains of West Virginia. How I got there and why I was there made absolutely no sense at all. Now, I can tell you that the Lord took me there to bring me to a place of understanding the importance of abiding in the mountain of God.

While in the mountains of West Virginia, the Lord both hid me and showed me the way of the Lord. In His time, He began to reveal to me new instructions, new ways, and new principles that I would have to choose to live by. God placed me in the mountains to get me all alone. This assured that as I moved in a new direction I was on my way to His new place. I was now going His direction and transitioned to a dimension of being totally dependent upon God alone.

I finally discovered the truth of Psalm 27: 5; for in the time of trouble He shall hide me in His pavilion. While in the mountains of West Virginia, I discovered many secrets of the Lord. These secret things clearly showed me His way, His principles, and His instructions for my life. I discovered the following principles in which I will always remember – you should as well:

- You are never alone, God is always with you.
- You have a great and high calling upon your life.
- God alone is everything – keeper, provider, and way maker.

The mountains of West Virginia possessed such a tremendous metaphor. It was a place of great serenity, quietness, and peacefulness. But also the mountains possessed the potential for incredible danger within all its gracefulness. I discovered this while driving through the mountains on a rainy afternoon. The rain had made the driving conditions extremely treacherous. While driving to church, my car came inches away from going over the mountain. I was inches from death yet I was safe. God taught me a lesson that I want to share with you as you journey through your mountain of God. The mountain of the Lord has in it the potential for life or death – it all depends on the way in which you make your way through the mountain.

The mountain of God must be preceded through using all the Godly wisdom you now possess. If your footing is not secure or you are driving in rainy conditions, you have the potential to be lost forever. While you are being brought through the mountain of God, your every step should be ordered by the Lord. The security is in your complete obedience! (II Corinthians 10: 6)

Some of you reading this book have taken greats falls and suffered much loss during this last season of abiding in the mountain of the Lord. You made it through the dark night but now it seems you cannot make any progress to get you to your next place in destiny. In fact, it seems you have lost more ground than you gained. Be encouraged you will make it out of the mountain of God. You will continue to make further progress and you will come to the place called promise land.

16 For a righteous man may fall seven times and rise again, but the wicked shall fall by calamity. (Proverbs 24: 16)

Take courage, you will not be utterly cast down. The

mountain of the Lord is designed to bring you to and through this very place in which you now stand. You must allow God's grace to sustain you through it all. There is nothing in God or in the mountain of the Lord created to destroy you. The heights, the depths, and the trickery of the mountains are designed to test you and more importantly, make you. Trust God like never before because He is the one who created the mountain. Stay focused for God will speak new words of life and will encourage you to keep going on to destiny.

Regardless of what you are experiencing right now, you can make it out of! Whether it is a bad marriage or negative relationship, or financial loss – you can recover. You can be healed; you can be delivered; you can be set free forever! It is going to be seen in the mountain of God (Genesis 22: 14). In this moment be alert, God is beginning to speak again. God has you in His mountain. He will keep you here until He has cleared the passage for you to move further (Joshua 2: 22)! Please be patient, God is not through with you yet.

> **16 Then Jacob awoke from his sleep and said, surely the Lord is in this place, and I did not know it.**
> **17 And he was afraid and said how awesome this place is! This is none other than the house of God, and this is the gate of heaven. (Genesis 28: 16, 17)**

This is the mountain of God! How awesome is this place – this is the house of God! In this place you shall discover God's great mercy and more of God's great grace. You will receive and understand the power and unlimited favor He has for His chosen new breed of leaders. When you have abided in this mountain, you will exit out knowing your calling and understanding of God's perfect will for your life. You shall declare you have survived the dark nights and journeyed through the mountain of God. You will be ready to rule over nations and kingdoms. You have now truly experienced the mountain of God.

17 And let the beauty of the Lord our God be upon us; and establish thou the work of our hands for us; yes, establish the work of our hands. (Psalm 90: 17)

nights and journeyed through the mountain of God. You will be ready to rule over nations and kingdoms. You have now truly experienced the mountain of God.

17 And let the beauty of the Lord our God be upon us; and establish thou the work of our hands for us; yes, establish the work of our hands. (Psalm 90: 17)

Chapter 5

"A new breed of chosen Leaders ready to Possess THE LAND of promise!"

Then the seventh angel sounded: And there were loud voices in heaven, saying, "The kingdoms of this world have become the kingdoms of our Lord and of His Christ, and He shall reign forever and ever!"

Revelation 11: 15

25 So the two men returned, and descended from the mountain; and passed over, and came to Joshua, the son of Nun, and told him all the things that befallen them.

26 And they said unto Joshua, truly the Lord hath delivered into our hands all the land; for even the inhabitants of the land do faint because of us. (Joshua 2: 23, 24)

Now you know and understand that the dark night had to be ventured through. You were destined to scale the high mountain for you to arrive at this place called destiny. This place is where you are ready to begin possessing the land of promise. You and many of your company of leaders are now beginning to possess your lands of promise because of your navigation through the dark night season. You have grown both character and strength that others will be willing to follow. You are now empowered and able to empower others for the journeys ahead of them. You understand the importance of abiding in the mountain of God.

Just as the two spies returned and reported to Joshua that Israel was ready to conqueror the city of Jericho, so shall you begin to proclaim to Church leadership that the promise lands are ready to be conquered by the Kingdom of God! You shall proclaim this to everyone that will hear your message. The promise land shall be possessed by the people of God. He has been waiting for His children to rise up and possess the land of promise.

Understand the precedents for a new breed like you abiding in mountain of God. Let's look at a few. First, there is Abraham who climbed a great mountain to discover the God who provides in Genesis 22. While Abraham stood on the mountain ready to sacrifice all, his God began to speak again a second time. Then there is Jacob who wrestled through the night to become the prince of Israel. He came out of the night having power with God and men. Finally, there is Moses standing on the backside of the desert. He stood in the dark and he climbed the mountain of God to become the leader of the nation of Israel. He stands on the mountain and receives an encounter with the face of God (Exodus 3). His face-to-face encounter with God, in the mountain of God, commissioned his leadership and caused all of Israel to be freed from the oppression of over four hundred years.

All these great men went through the same encounter you have just journeyed through, dark nights and the mountain of the Lord. Just as they came out new and began to change their world for the better, so shall you...you shall rise up as a new breed of chosen leaders – Isaiah 58: 12!

The two spies returned to Joshua and declared that the promise land was ready to be possessed by the children of Israel. They gave Joshua an update informing him the land was theirs to be possessed. This was a new breed ready to embark upon and possess the land of promise.

As you read this, I want you to understand that there was nothing experienced in the night or in the mountain that discouraged them from continuing to move forward. In fact, everything they had experienced caused their faith in God to grow. They believed everything God said was going to happened before their very eyes.

27 And they said unto Joshua, truly the Lord hath delivered into our hands all the land; for even all the inhabitants of the country do faint because of us. (Joshua 2: 24)

The two spies were thoroughly convinced of the greatness and unlimited power of their God. No one or nothing could possibly stand against them. They believed through it all that they were mightier than any of their enemies. This is a very important factor of your journey as you learn to walk by faith in God. This is what has determined that you shall possess the promise land – your great faith in God.

In essence, your great faith in God determines your possession of the promise land. The fresh experience of surviving the dark nights and scaling the very high mountain convinced the spies that nothing was impossible with God.

This thing called doubt is now out of your life forever! The last generation of leaders walked through life doubting the God they served. But you are of the new breed that shall rise up and lead others into walking by faith. You are now sure that your God is more than enough. What you have gone through has birthed new faith, new confidence and new strength!

Your intense struggles through the dark nights and the very high mountain shall be your testimony of what God is really able to do. Your great faith and God's divine ability shall encourage and lead others not to be hindered or impeded by minor obstacles or insignificant distractions. Every test and battle ahead will be navigated through by your unyielding faith in God.

Just as God moved on behalf of Joshua, these two spies, and all of the camp of Israel, He is ready to move for you and the leaders standing by your side. Nothing can overwhelm you as you possess the land of promise. God has made you more than conquerors. He has positioned you directly in the place of possessing your promise land. Yes, it truly is right ahead of you. Even when you are standing still, God is giving you the land of promise.

You must now complete the task of possessing the promise land. You have everything that you will need. You shall discover while you were purposely moving through the dark nights and over the high mountains God has added to your life. You have great faith, additional strength, and the proven ability. Even when you stand still, you will see the salvation of the Lord your God. He has declared that you are ready and able to possess your promise land. God shall be strong in battle with you as you fight courageously to acquire every inch of the promise land. God is rising in you and all your enemies are scattering (Psalm 68: 1).

13 Thou shalt arise, and have mercy upon Zion: for the time to favor her, yea, the set time has come. (Psalm 102: 13)

You shall discover the enemies are no longer standing as they stood before. You have entered into and you are on your way to possessing! Your enemies are decreasing in strength. Each time you look you shall see them getting smaller and smaller. They are bread for you and their defense is gone. You are on your way to conquering all of the promise land. What does it mean to possess the land? It means all of the following:

- Every word of the Lord spoken concerning you, your family, and all those connected to you will begin to come to pass.
- Those enemies in the land that have prevented God's plan from coming to pass are expelled out of the land. Enemies like depression, murder, and poverty are all removed from the land.
- Obedience to God's written word and spoken promises are the order of the day for all those that occupy the land of promise.
- The will of the Lord is clearly seen in the moment.
- Everything manifests that God declares shall manifest.

It is now time! You are ready and the land of promise is ready. You will see things come to pass that God has promised you days ago. Your waiting is over. No more delays and no more denials.

Nations and kingdoms shall rise up out of thee and assist you in possessing the land of promise. You are now a representative and leader of the Kingdom of God – God's kingdom is advancing through you! The agenda is to possess all the land of promise – the whole earth (Psalm 24: 1, 2)! All this and more is about to be seen by you and the entire world. You are armed, you are ready, and the captain of the Lord's host goes before you (Joshua 5). Whatever you believe and all that you speak shall occur. So you must walk in the wisdom of God. God is with you and His angels are working on your behalf.

You will only say exactly what God says – it's time to possess the land of promise! You have risen into another place, now declare it from this place – it's time to possess the land of promise! Declare it, declare it, speak it, speak it with all of your might – it's time to possess the land of promise! Forget what's behind you and begin pressing into those things that are before you – the great land of promise (Philippians 4: 13).

Now have experienced and now you understand the importance of abiding in the mountain of God!

Chapter 6

A Word of the Lord...
"The Season of transition is here!"

A word spoken fitly is like apples of gold in pictures of silver.

Proverbs 25: 11

*T*here is a new breed of chosen leaders positioned, poised, and prepared to lead the kingdom of God. They will lead into possessing all of the promise land! They have made it through the dark nights and have traveled into and out of the mountain of God. They are shifting swiftly into positions of leadership. They are leading in many places and many positions. They are being entrusted with great influence and authority. Their names being known are not very important. They are more focused on completing their assignment than gaining personal recognition. They are the leaders that will touch men, women, children, nations, and kingdoms of this world. They are leaders which have matured and they are ready to take dominion in the earth.

These leaders have the knowledge of what needs to be done in these pivotal times and how to make crucial decisions. They are like the tribe of Issachar spoken of in II Chronicles 12: 32. These leaders move by the prophetic word of the Lord. They are prophetic people by nature. They do not run in the face of opposition. They do not fear the face of men. They have received their commission from the Lord God. They understand order and submission to the powers that be. However, they stand secure before the Lord their God. They stand before Him both day and night! They are the new breed of chosen leaders ready to lead many others through the mountain of our God. They are a new breed of leaders.

November 30, 2006
This is a word from the Lord concerning this group of new breed chosen leaders. Thus says the Lord, "It will not profit for men, organizations, or nations to stand against these servants of the Lord God. They are now taking the lead in position and post of major influence. To fight against them is to fight against the Lord (St. Matthew 23: 29-31). These leaders carry the present knowledge, wis-

dom, and judgments of the Lord! Their assignment is to speak and reveal the heart of the Lord God. When God speaks, they speak; when God is quiet, they are quiet; when God says advance, they advance. God has raised these new breed of chosen leaders up to lead another generation into the things of the Lord. God is revealing the deep and secret things to this new breed of chosen leaders. In the present shift, present and old leaders will be replaced. God shall now establish His house with a group of faithful priests, faithful prophets, and faithful servant-kings. God is choosing a group of leaders that will have clean hands and a pure heart. Some leaders already in positions of great influence will attempt to keep the order of the day and try to keep things business as usual. But this will cause God to judge them swiftly (Romans 11: 22)! God will have a new breed of chosen leaders that will build other men and women for the Kingdom of God. God has come to set His people totally free. Leadership must have a desire to see God get all the glory to remain in positions of influence. All the things that were birthed of the self-will must be removed (Proverbs 19: 21). Leaders are now under God's mandate to get the things of the Lord right! Leadership will get it right or they shall be removed. The Church (the Body of Christ) must now be prepared for change and transition.

In the midst of all these leadership changes, God shall rise up and establish a faithful people. These people will be much like the great prophet Samuel of old. There will be masses of people moving like one big army of the Lord (Joel 2: 1-11). This army is not coming to take sides but they are coming to take over. The Lord warns you all again: do not attempt to harm, speak against, or sway this group. They are totally committed to the Lord their God. They are marching to the orders of their king, the Lord God. God shall bless those that bless them and God shall curse those that attempt to curse them. God's mighty hand is upon them to perform His strange acts.

God is ready to take His people (The Body of Christ- The Church) into its final dimension! These new breed of chosen leaders will be the key component in moving the entire earth into this place of promise. They now come pronouncing the way of the Lord and the way in which you and I must take!

To You – A New Breed of Leaders

I speak to you reading this book – know the Lord's hand is upon you. Rise up and take your place! It is now time for you to lead! Go and the Lord your God goes with you. You cannot be hindered neither will you be stopped. There is a group in heaven and a group on the earth cheering for you (Hebrews 11). Please keep going until the battle has been won!

I must release you for now, but I am praying for each of you. You must understand what has happened while you have been abiding in the mountain. Everything has transitioned and everything has changed – including you! You have been prepared for the last great battle between good and evil, and you are prepared to lead the people of the Most High God, nations, and kingdoms. The voice of the Lord God has spoken. You have received your instructions. God is now waiting on your response.

The time for you to depart is swiftly approaching. You must part in order to finish the remainder of your journey. Move forward listening closely for the voice of the Lord your God. From here you will at times abide in the mountain of God! Other times you will be required to depart from the mountain that you may lead others back into the mountain. Know that every morning God's mercies are anew, His grace is sufficient, and His goodness is everlasting. I leave you with these final words. Live life committed to your purpose; consistently depend on your relationship with God; and refuse to die until you have completed all that God has predestined for you to do.

32 Those who do wickedly against the covenant he shall corrupt with flattery; but the people who know their God shall be strong, and carry out great exploits. (Daniel 11: 32)

CPSIA information can be obtained at www.ICGtesting.com
Printed in the USA
LVOW061255200412

278410LV00001B/279/P